MOTORCYCLE ON PATROL

THE STORY OF A HIGHWAY OFFICER
by JOAN HEWETT

photographs by
RICHARD HEWETT

CLARION BOOKS
TICKNOR & FIELDS: A HOUGHTON MIFFLIN COMPANY
NEW YORK

From coast to coast state law enforcement agencies safeguard the nation's highways. This book looks at one such agency, the California Highway Patrol, and focuses on one of its officers, Fermin Piol (pronounced *Pea-ol*). We want to thank the California Highway Patrol for making this book possible. For their specific cooperation we'd like to recognize: Captain William P. Carlson, commander of the California Highway Patrol academy, and Captain Richard L. Lane, commander of the South Los Angeles area, and the men and women in their commands. A special thanks also goes to Officer Richard Richards and Officer Fermin Piol for their steadfast help. Thanks also go to the Goodhew Ambulance Service for their cooperation.

Clarion Books
Ticknor & Fields, a Houghton Mifflin Company
Text copyright © 1986 by Joan Hewett
Photographs copyright © 1986 by Richard Hewlett
All rights reserved. Printed in the U.S.A.

HO 10 9 8 7 6 5 4 3 2 1

Library of Congress Cataloging-in-Publication Data
Hewett, Joan.
Motorcycle on patrol
Includes index.
Summary: Follows a highway patrol officer through his training
as a motorcycle officer and his first few weeks on the job.
1. Traffic police—California—Juvenile literature.
[1. Traffic police. 2. Police. 3. Motorcycling. 4. Occupations]
I. Hewett, Richard, ill. II. Title.
HV8079.5.H48   1986   363.2′332   86-2689
ISBN 0-89919-372-2

CONTENTS

1. ON PATROL: AN 11-79

Cutting through the static, the dispatcher's voice comes over the car radio, "LA 77–40, there's an 11–79 on the northbound Harbor Freeway, north of the Torrance on-ramp."

Officer Fermin Piol listens intently: 77–40 is his car, 11–79 stands for Accident—Ambulance Rolling. Microphone in hand, Fermin radios back that he and his partner, Officer Toni Williams, are on their way. It is 5:40 P.M. Officer Williams enters the time in her activity log. Emergency lights flashing, siren blaring, the California Highway Patrol (CHP) car heads toward the nearby freeway.

Moments later the freeway is in sight. Traffic is heavy. Fermin's jaw clenches. If he were on a motorcycle, he'd ride straight and fast between the cars. Maybe if he's accepted for the next motorcycle training session...But he hasn't been yet, and he may not be. The

freeway on-ramp is coming up fast. Fermin cuts his thoughts short and turns off the siren and emergency lights. Drivers would have to switch lanes to make way for his car, and on a crowded freeway that could cause confusion and accidents.

Now with the skill of a veteran officer, Fermin weaves through the traffic "unseen." His concentration doesn't waver. He watches the cars. He listens to the two-way radio in case the dispatcher has more news of the accident.

Over 750 miles of freeway grid Los Angeles County. It's the job of CHP officers to patrol those roads and safeguard the more than 3.5 million people who use them daily. Traffic flow is monitored at the Traffic Operations Center (TOC), which is run by the CHP and the California Department of Transportation.

9

The center's closed-circuit TV receivers show key sections of the freeway system. Varied lights on an electronic wall-sized map indicate how fast traffic is moving. This information comes from electronic devices in the road's surface. A line of blinking lights on the map means that traffic is backing up and coming to a standstill. Has there been an accident? A CHP officer is radioed to check it out.

Other accidents, like the one Fermin and Toni are responding to, are reported by motorists from roadside emergency phones. The calls are answered at the CHP's Los Angeles Communication Center, and they are instantly routed to the proper dispatcher.

Dispatchers are assigned to, and stay in continual radio contact with, the officers who patrol a particular city area. Seated at individual computerized consoles, the dispatchers direct their officers to traffic problems, supply them with vehicle or driver information, and summon needed aid: fire truck, ambulance, tow truck or clean-up crew.

It was the South Los Angeles dispatcher who routed Fermin and Toni to the accident. They should be there soon. She waits to hear.

On the freeway, traffic slows abruptly. Using his emergency lights, Fermin zigs across the lanes, while Toni radios in a 10–97: Arrived at Scene.

Two cars have collided. Fermin parks behind them to shield them from being hit by oncoming traffic. The man and woman who are standing near one of the cars seem unhurt. Fermin turns a spotlight on the other car.

There is a driver slumped over the steering wheel. He is dazed, unsure of what has happened. Fermin tells him not to move and assures him that he'll be all right. An ambulance is on the way.

Because an ambulance and paramedic can normally reach any section of the Los Angeles freeway system in minutes, officers who patrol it only treat the seriously wounded when seconds might make a difference.

Moving quickly Fermin grabs a handful of flares from the patrol car trunk. Help won't be able to get through until he can get and keep the traffic rolling.

Toni has radioed for a tow truck and told the two people, who are now safely by the side of the road, to stay where they are. Then she joins Fermin. Like a lighted rope the flares separate the traffic from the accident. Watching out for problems, the two officers wave the cars and trucks on.

13

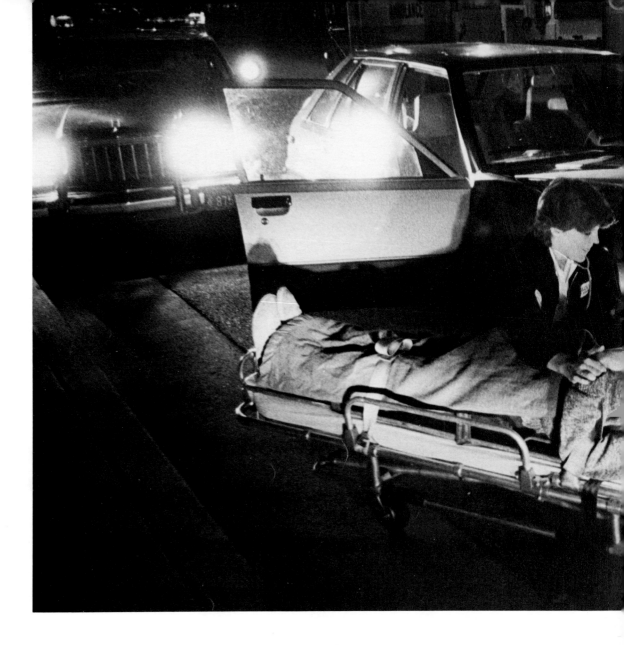

Before four minutes have passed, Fermin spots the ambulance and directs it over. The paramedic springs out. She examines and treats the injured man. Then Fermin questions him briefly about the accident, checks his driver's license, and records the information. The man is transferred to the ambulance.

Now Toni questions the couple who were involved and takes down their statements. Examining the physical evidence at the scene is

Fermin's job. He inspects the cars. Are the headlights on and working? Are the tires worn? He checks for skid marks and measures them.

Soon the tow truck arrives.

Thirty-two minutes have elapsed since Fermin and Toni received the injury-accident report. All the other people and vehicles are gone. Fermin gathers up the last of the flares. Toni radios in a 10–98: Assignment Completed. They are back on patrol.

For close to two years, Fermin has worked this shift and driven this beat. But tonight, almost against his will, he finds himself thinking about motorcycle training.

Even when he was going through the CHP academy, he knew that he'd want to be a motor officer someday. But it hadn't seemed pressing. Not then. Not when he was on the verge of becoming a law enforcement officer, for being an officer was something he'd thought about from the time he was seven years old.

"Who would like to be a crossing guard?" his second grade teacher had asked, and Fermin had volunteered. Letting the other kids know when they could and couldn't cross was fun. He started noticing real officers, police and highway patrolmen and women, and he wondered what it would be like to be one. Then when he was older, motorcycles and cars fascinated him. After a while he began to think about the highway patrol as a career. He took law enforcement classes in college. The idea of being on his own, taking responsibility, making on-the-spot decisions was appealing. A law enforcement career was for him!

The CHP was his first choice. More than ten thousand men and women applied at the same time he did. There were written exams, a personal interview, and a physical exam. Fermin could hardly believe his good fortune when he was one of the two hundred applicants chosen for training.

At the CHP Academy in Sacramento, California, Fermin and the other cadets went through a twenty-week, semi-military training course. They were drilled and tested in defensive driving, self-defense, marksmanship, as well as first aid and cardiopulmonary resuscitation (CPR), a heart revival method. Weight training, calisthenics and track built up their strength, flexibility, and endurance. They learned laws of arrest, court procedures, rules of the road, search and seizure laws and more.

Upon graduation Fermin was assigned to the South Los Angeles area office. New officers are car patrol officers. During their first year they are closely supervised and are not eligible for special duty or training. Fermin put in his request for motorcycle training as soon as the year was over. Many officers who were his senior wanted to become motor officers, so he was prepared for a long wait.

Still, the more time that went by, the more Fermin wanted to be a motor officer. And then Fermin heard that a South Los Angeles car officer would be chosen for academy motorcycle training to replace an officer who was leaving.

Fermin knew that his sergeant had recommended him. He knew the next training session started in ten days. He expected to hear— soon.

As tonight's shift comes to an end, Fermin and Toni report back to the office. They chat with other returning officers, and Fermin pours himself a cup of coffee. Patrol officers, even those who work the same shift, spend little time together. They see officers other than their own partner when they report for their daily briefing, and again eight hours later when the shift ends. Even so, there is a close bond among them. They are graduates of the same academy; they are the best, and they are doing a tough, demanding job. Hardly a week goes by when an officer doesn't need or respond to the call for help from another officer.

Now Fermin looks over his accident report, draws a diagram of the collision and writes his conclusion: what he thinks the cause or causes were.

Accident report information is fed into a central computer and analyzed. The CHP can tell how many accidents take place in California daily, which freeways have the most accidents, and which have the fewest. They can judge how well new equipment or new regulations, like a reduced speed limit, work.

Next Fermin checks his activity log to be sure that the entries are legible. Like all CHP officers, Fermin spends far more time helping motorists than citing them for violations. And every time he stops, whether it's to give directions, or to push a stalled car to the side of the road, he enters it in his log.

Fermin finishes, then starts toward the locker room. One of his fellow officers calls, "Hey, Fermin, Sergeant Lawrence wants you."

This has to be it! Fermin thinks. *The academy's decision.*

The sergeant is seated behind his desk. He stands and holds out his hand in congratulations. And soon every officer there is pounding Fermin on the back, kidding him, and wishing him good luck.

2. MOTORCYCLE TRAINING

The campus looks just the way he remembers it—well ordered and somehow special. Suitcase and boots in hand, he heads toward the dorms. Check in Sunday after 2:00 P.M., his instructions had said. Bring proper-style boots that protect the ankles, CHP coveralls, gloves, glasses or sunglasses, and Sam Browne belt with weapons. The special belt, which is designed to carry weapons, is named for its inventor, the British general, Sir Samuel James Browne.

The next morning the trainees are edgy as they walk to class. The two-week motorcycle course rapidly weeds out those officers who do not have what it takes. Half the trainees in a class may fail. It's no disgrace. They can take the course again in a few years, and of course they are still officers.

An instructor introduces himself. Then he swings the chalkboard into place. "What we're going to teach you is called enforcement riding, but what you're actually going to learn is how to stay alive.

"You're all good officers, that's why you've been chosen. Some of you know how to ride a bike. That probably means you have some bad habits, and we'll do our best to make sure you lose them. And of course, those of you who have no motorcycle experience won't do as well as those who do, at first. But right now, we're going to get you ready to ride."

Fermin and his classmates learn the names of a motorcycle's parts and what all the parts do. Then they are off to practice shifting.

23

The trainees take turns shifting on a bike that is up on a block. Then they practice the correct way to lift a 600-pound bike. "If you don't use your leg muscles, you'll hurt your back," the instructor warns. Trying on helmets is next. Then every trainee picks out a motorcycle, walks it over to the gas pumps, and fills it up. It's time to start! A thundering *vroom vroom* fills the air. They run their bikes along a short flat road, where the trainees that need help are coached.

Then right after lunch they line up on their bikes behind an instructor and ride off at a slow pace.

When they reach the motorcycle courses, the instructor says, "You'll be learning precision riding by going through a series of exercises. You'll be graded on each exercise and you'll receive your grades daily. My advice is don't share them with anyone. What matters is how well you are doing and how much you are improving."

Riding cone patterns comes first. Sometimes the cones are evenly spaced, sometimes they are spaced randomly. The trainees weave through them very slowly, at three to five miles per hour. The exercises give the rider a feel for the bike and develop balance and rhythm.

There are two instructors. One instructor describes an exercise and explains how it's done. He points out what the body should be doing, where the riders should be looking, and even what they should be thinking. The other instructor rides through the course a couple of times, so they can see how it is done.

Fermin goes through the patterns carefully and without mishap. Then the speed is increased, and he knocks over two cones. He's angry and tells himself he'll do it perfectly next time. But there is no next time. The trainees ride through a pattern two or three times and then go on to a different one that requires the same body movement and clutch-throttle coordination. Fermin stops worrying about past slip-ups and concentrates on doing his best.

They receive advice. "Lean into a pattern more, don't lean so much. Pull your clutch in, let it out. Don't look at your fender, don't look at the cones, look where you're going."

As the days go by they practice ninety-degree turns, U-turns, S-turns and figure eights. When most of the class can execute a U-turn in seventeen feet, then it's time to do it in sixteen feet, then fifteen…. "Don't look at the wall, it isn't going anywhere," an instructor says. "Look down the road. Cheat a little, turn your wheel slightly before you turn."

By the end of the week, the trainees are going through the exercises with greater precision and at a much faster pace. They practice braking and learn how to stop quickly without sliding their wheels and losing steering control.

"No one has fallen yet," an instructor comments just before they break for the weekend. "Now maybe you're all that good; or maybe you're playing it safe, too safe, because you're afraid to fall. Just remember you're going to need the techniques that we're teaching you to enforcement ride. And if you don't learn them, you won't be a motor officer."

Monday of the second week arrives. Fermin squirms in his classroom seat. There are, by his calculations, only forty more hours of training, and he doesn't want to spend part of them learning rules and regulations.

Finally they don helmets, glasses, and gloves. "You won't have it so easy from now on," an instructor says. And it *is* rougher. They ride up and down hills, turn on inclines, and practice broadslides, skids, and emergency stops.

Dirt flies and splatters, and almost every trainee falls—lays his bike down.

Fermin roars up an incline, but on the way down he locks his back brakes. The bike bucks and Fermin hits the dirt. He's bruised but okay.

By midweek Fermin thinks he's got a good chance of getting through the course successfully. His grades aren't great, but they're all right. *Now if I can only hang in there,* he tells himself.

There's a written exam on motorcycle rules, regulations, and procedures, and another on motorcycle maintenance. On paved double-lane roads they practice "partner-riding": riding side by side with another officer and switching lanes without breaking their pace. And now toward the end of each day, one of their instructors will say, "Follow me." Then single file they ride across and along courses, fields, roads, and hills going fast and faster. It's fun!

Suddenly there is no time for "tomorrow I'll do better" thoughts. It's Friday. Fermin's nervous, more nervous than he can remember being. Then he gets news. He's passed! He's a certified, Class I motorcycle rider.

3. MARY MEANS MOTORCYCLE

Back in South Los Angeles, Fermin's motorcycle is waiting for him. The bike isn't new, but it's in top condition. He washes and polishes it, then changes into his motorcycle uniform.

CHP officers take their bikes home. When they ride back and forth between home and office, they are officially on duty and must be in full uniform.

Fermin's gold and blue helmet with its winged motorcycle symbol, his black boots, tan riding pants, matching shirt with its CHP insignia, and his official brass badge, quickly identify him as a CHP officer. His helmet and boots also protect him from injury. So do his gloves and shatterproof glasses.

For the first month a new officer rides with, and is supervised by, a motorcycle training officer. Although it seldom happens, the training officer could decide that the new officer can't hack it. Then he, or she, would return to car patrol.

Fermin isn't worried about his ability. He was a good car patrol officer. He'll be an even better motor officer. Patroling with an experienced motor officer will give him a sound start.

They ride side by side.

Fermin watches for motorists who need help, dangerous drivers who might cause accidents, unsafe vehicles, road obstacles and possible stolen vehicles. There's a CHP radio behind Fermin's seat and a speaker and mike on his instrument panel. His helmet is also equipped with a speaker and an extending mike. This small but powerful system lets Fermin communicate with the dispatcher and still have his hands free to gear up and down, brake, or operate his lights and police signals: front red flashers, rear yellow flashers, and siren. Unlike most motorcyclists, CHP officers don't have to ride with their lights on, and they often turn them off when approaching a suspicious vehicle.

Fermin observes the other officer. He notices how he hand signals. He also takes note of how many feet he stops behind an offending van, at what angle he parks his bike, and how quickly he gets off it and onto his feet.

After the first week, the officer will often give Fermin a "this one is yours" sign when they spot a speeding or dangerous driver. Fermin rapidly learns that his reflexes must be fast, his judgment accurate. Before signaling a driver to pull over, he must be sure that he can fol-

low the driver and shield the vehicle from oncoming traffic without endangering himself. He no longer has a car around him to act as a buffer.

Sometimes the officer will explain to Fermin what he might have done differently, and why. He also cautions Fermin about pursuit. "Don't ride over your head. Sure, you've got the power to do more than a hundred miles per hour. But that doesn't mean you should take the same risks that some crazy drunk or car thief takes. Call in. Get help."

By the end of the month Fermin feels confident. He's ready to patrol on his own.

At today's briefing Fermin will get his new assignment. He dresses with care and makes sure that his holster, handgun and extra bullets, his handcuffs as well as handcuff and motorcycle keys are all fastened to his Sam Browne belt. CHP officers use their weapons only in life-threatening situations, but they are part of their uniform and must be worn. Then he checks his bike's utility boxes. *Vehicle Code* book, ticket books, arrest and accident forms, tag books (so he can flag deserted vehicles), street map, flares, first-aid kit, flashlight and tourniquet are all there.

Fermin arrives early for the briefing. He waits. Finally Sergeant Lawrence strides in. Beat assignments are somewhat fixed, because officers patrol a beat best when they are familiar with it. They must know which freeway exits are dangerous at high speeds, which intersections flood in a downpour, which deserted streets drag racers race…

Now the sergeant names each beat and the officer or officers who are assigned to it. Fermin listens, "...85 Mary, Officer Trumbull; 66 Mary, Officer Smith; 110 Mary, Officer Piol..." That's it! His new beat. From now on his designation will be LA 77–110 Mary. LA 77 stands for South Los Angeles, 110 stands for his beat, and Mary means motorcycle.

Next Sergeant Lawrence goes over traffic control information. On-going freeway repairs will slow traffic, a rock concert may cause traffic congestion. Then the sergeant glares at them. Car accidents in South Los Angeles are on the rise, he reports sharply.

Emphasizing each word, the sergeant continues, "We're going to start reversing that statistic right now. You know that ninety percent of all drivers who are cited for reckless driving are under the influence of alcohol or drugs. That means there are a lot of drunks on the roads, and you're not getting them."

Excited and proud Fermin patrols his new beat. Like his old beat, this one includes both freeway and city streets. As Fermin rides he notices the names of the streets. He looks at the people, the houses and storefronts, and keeps an eye out for signs of vandalism or gang activity. When he pulls up alongside a car at a light, he automatically glances inside. In one car a lone driver is bobbing her head oddly. He watches, and realizes she's keeping time to music. Then Fermin spots a car with a broken side window. There are four people inside, plus the driver. Had they broken into the car, then driven it away?

Fermin "runs the car": he gives the dispatcher the car's color, year, make, body type and license number. He follows the car closely until the dispatcher reports "no wants."

For the next few hours Fermin rides his beat uneventfully. Then he receives an 11–84: Direct Traffic. A produce truck has overturned

on the freeway spilling its cargo. Two lanes are blocked and traffic is backed up. *But why should it be backed up this far*, Fermin wonders. And then he sees why. A car has stalled. The driver tells Fermin she thinks she can make it over to the shoulder and be out of the way.

Fermin diverts traffic for her. Then once she's over, he cautions her to stay in the car and radios for a tow truck. Now he must undo the traffic snarl. Standing out on the freeway, he directs the trucks, cars and buses holding back some, and letting others go.

Returning to his bike, Fermin patrols at a steady pace. A car keeps drifting across its lane. Is the driver talking? Fermin moves up to get a closer look. There are no passengers. Suddenly the car's front wheels turn sharply. Fermin changes lanes so he's right behind the car. Sure enough, the car, without signaling, turns off the freeway, speeds down the ramp, and runs a light.

Fermin keeps the car in view, catches up, and signals the driver over. Then he radios the dispatcher his location and requests that she 10–23: Stand By.

Is the man dangerous? Is he armed? Fermin approaches on foot. His eyes rake the man's face and figure and the inside of the car. The man's head is bowed. There are no signs of weapons, drugs, or alcohol.

"Did you see the light?" Fermin asks. "Were you rushing to get somewhere? Is this your car?" The man finally responds. His speech is slurred, his breath smells of alcohol, and when Fermin asks him to take his driver's license out of his wallet, his fingers fumble.

Fermin thinks the driver is drunk. Now he must confirm this suspicion by testing the man's coordination and balance. He frisks the man for concealed weapons and proceeds.

44

The man can't focus his eyes and follow Fermin's moving finger. He can't raise one foot a few inches from the ground without losing his balance. And when Fermin tells him to hold his hands behind his back and walk heel-to-toe in a straight line, he lurches from side to side.

Fermin handcuffs the man, then informs him that he'll have to submit to a chemical test to determine the alcoholic content of his blood. "I've got a 10–15": Prisoner in Custody, he tells the waiting dispatcher.

Soon a highway patrol car arrives and the officer takes the prisoner in tow.

Fermin enters the incident in his log and checks the time. How can it be? He has looked forward to this day for so long, and now his shift is almost over. Then Fermin laughs at his disappointment. Why there will be weeks, months, and years of motorcycle patrol ahead!

He radios in a 10–98: Assignment Completed. He starts his engine. LA 77–110 Mary is back on patrol.

INDEX